Drive and Stroll in

West Yorkshire

Ron Freethy

COUNTRYSIDE BOOKS
NEWBURY BERKSHIRE

COUNTRYSIDE BOOKS
3 Catherine Road
Newbury, Berkshire

To view our complete range of books,
please visit us at
www.countrysidebooks.co.uk

ISBN 978 1 85306 980 2

The cover picture shows the
view towards Rombalds Moor
supplied by Bill Meadows

Photographs by the author
Maps by Gelder Design & Mapping
Designed by Peter Davies, Nautilus Design

Produced through MRM Associates Ltd., Reading
Typeset by CJWT Solutions, St Helens
Printed by Cambridge University Press

.

Contents

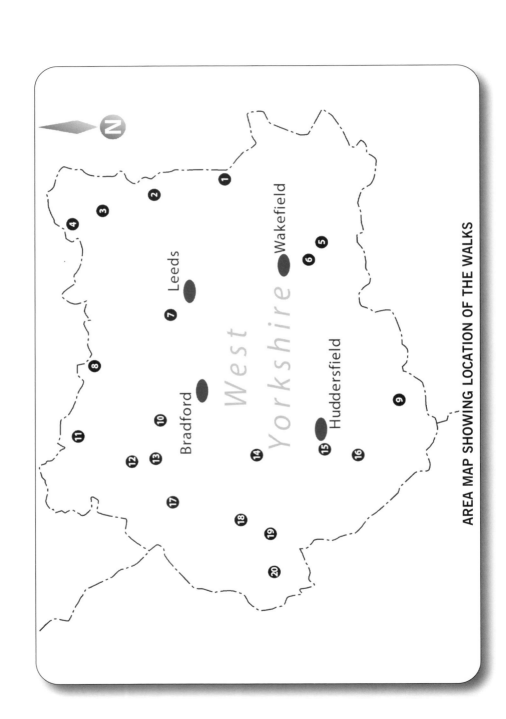

AREA MAP SHOWING LOCATION OF THE WALKS

Contents

PUBLISHER'S NOTE

We hope that you obtain considerable enjoyment from this book; great care has been taken in its preparation. Although at the time of publication all routes followed public rights of way or permitted paths, diversion orders can be made and permissions withdrawn.

We cannot, of course, be held responsible for such diversion orders and any inaccuracies in the text which result from these or any other changes to the routes nor any damage which might result from walkers trespassing on private property. We are anxious though that all details covering the walks are kept up to date and would therefore welcome information from readers which would be relevant to future editions.

The simple sketch maps that accompany the walks in this book are based on notes made by the author whilst checking out the routes on the ground. However, for the benefit of a proper map, we do recommend that you purchase the relevant Ordnance Survey sheet covering your walk. The Ordnance Survey maps are widely available, especially through booksellers and local newsagents.

Introduction

It is more than 30 years since I began walking in West Yorkshire and enjoying its wonderful combination of history, natural history and unique industrial archaeology, so having to select just twenty walks was a bit of a problem. But my choice had to include the first nature reserve in the world at Walton, and one of nature's miracles which has seen the RSPB's Fairburn Ings reserve created from massive coalfield subsidence. Other routes travel along the old packhorse routes around Hebden Bridge and Heptonstall, the causeways around Stoodley Pike and follow the old London Road which is now just a footpath. At Aberford I strolled from an old coaching inn and around some earthworks dating to the Iron Age.

Neither did I want to neglect the rich history and literary connections. It was a joy to follow in the footsteps of the Cistercian monks at Kirkstall, and enjoy the waterfalls so beloved by the Brontë sisters at Haworth. Another beautiful stroll was around Sandal Castle near Wakefield, where the ruins are set among glorious countryside.

Waterside walks are fascinating, and I found delightful strolls around the reservoirs at Blackmoorfoot and Scammonden. There is an abundance of riverside rambles in West Yorkshire, and I had to restrict myself to circular strolls around Wetherby, Otley and Ilkley. I found a splendid waterfall walk at Harden, near Bingley, as well as discovering a waterway walk around *Last of the Summer Wine* country.

The industrial archaeologist will find much to enjoy with the stroll around Shibden Hall providing reminders of the early days of the Industrial Revolution. Shibden itself is a splendid half-timbered hall set in many acres of parkland. The same applies to my stroll around Bramham. And the old mill at Saltaire, as well as being a reminder of the days of industry, is a lesson in the art of restoring the scars left by the textile age.

Drivers and strollers need a pleasant place to eat, so I sought out old coaching inns, riverside restaurants and even found a café situated within the 13th-century abbot's gatehouse at Kirkstall. At Scammonden I found what seems to be the oldest themed pub in Britain which was opened in 1935 using material from the liner *Mauritania*.

Sketch maps are included for each stroll, with numbered points that correspond with the numbered paragraphs in the text, but it is wise to carry with you the relevant Ordnance Survey Explorer map, details of which are provided. Suggestions are given for where to park, but, if parking in the car park of a pub or café, do always obtain the proprietor's permission if you wish to leave your car there while you do the stroll. Please use common sense wherever you park, and do not obstruct entrances or private parking places.

These gentle strolls vary in length between 2 and 6½ miles, and each proves what a beautiful county West Yorkshire is. I hope that they will both encourage local people to look at their home patch with renewed enthusiasm, and also show visitors what delights there are to be enjoyed. So everyone, of whatever age, polish up your boots and brush up your appetites.

Ron Freethy

The delightful countryside around Scammonden Water

1 Ledsham and Fairburn Ings

The RSPB reserve at Fairburn Ings

The Walk 5½ miles ⏱ 3-4 hours which allows leisure to enjoy the nature reserve.
Map: OS Explorer 289 (GR 455296)

How to get there

From the newly re-routed A1(T) follow the sign for Ledsham via a roundabout. Approach the village via Holyrood Lane. **Parking:** There is street parking around the village and a substantial car park for patrons of the Chequers. Care needs to be taken because there is a nearby village called Ledston which often causes confusion.

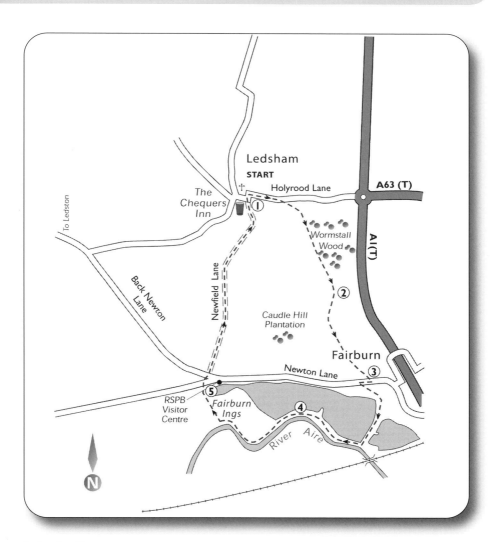

Introduction

This is a pleasant and gentle stroll through ancient history and impressive countryside. It leads around a substantial bird reserve created as a result of coal mining subsidence close to the River Aire. The nearby A1 seems many miles away and the wooded areas of this walk ring with bird song whilst the rich grassy areas are full of colourful flowers and the butterflies which feed upon their nectar.

Drive and Stroll

The Chequers Inn

There cannot be too many hostelries which still have only a six-day licence. Around 1830, the lady of the manor of Ledsham was on her way to church when she saw some of her workers lying drunk. She therefore decreed that the hostelry should be 'dry' on the Sabbath. Neither can there be many hostelries as welcoming as the Chequers. In cold weather the open fires and exposed beams welcome visitors of all ages. In pleasant weather, the beer garden is impressive and supplied with heaters close to the tables.

The menu is guaranteed to please gourmets and those who just need a quick snack before or after their walk. The Sunday closure strangely enough seems to add something to the history of the place. Telephone: 01977 683135.

THE WALK

Close to the Chequers Inn stands All Saints, one of the most impressive little churches to be found anywhere in Britain. It is of Anglo-Saxon foundation and dates to the 8th century. A Norman tower was constructed on top of a Saxon base and there are also clear examples of pre-Conquest carving. Although restored during the Victorian period, substantial sections of the original church were untouched.

①

From the church take the road to the left and find a gate on the right. Turn through the gate and ascend an obvious path. This leads into and through **Wormstall Wood**.

 ②

Pass through a stile into another area of woodland. The path climbs gently and then approaches farm buildings. The route follows an obvious and wide track.

 ③

Descend to **Newton Lane**. Turn right on a footpath parallel to Newton Lane and keep a reed-fringed lake to the right. The path bears right and to the left is the **River Aire** with the **Fairburn Ings** lake to the right.

The lake was created as part of the restoration process, and it is hard to imagine that, just half a century ago, this area was dirty, dusty and devastated as a result of coal mining. The wounds of industry have now healed and the area has become one of the most famous bird-watching sites in Britain.

 ④

The route undulates along the now grassed-over old spoil heaps and passes a number of comfortable

The Anglo-Saxon church of All Saints, Ledsham

All Saints church viewed from the road

bird hides and areas set aside for bird-watching.

 ⑤

Approach the **RSPB Visitors Centre**. It is open daily from 10 am until 5 pm, and here you can find plenty of information about the reserve and the wildlife around. There is a shop and excellent toilet facilities. From the RSPB centre, approach a very minor road. Turn right and at a junction with another minor road, bear left and turn almost immediately right, close to a sign indicating **Ledston** (Note: not Ledsham) and **Kippax**. Do not follow this but take an obvious path through fields keeping a woodland to the left. The path gradually widens and leads back into **Ledsham**.

2 | Aberford

The church of St Ricarius in Aberford

The Walk 6 miles 🕐 Allow 3 hours
Map: OS Explorer 289 (GR 433373)

How to get there

Aberford is signed off Junction 45 of the A1(M), which itself is signed off the A64 linking York and Leeds. Although now isolated by these new roads, Aberford stands on a Roman road that was later one of the most important coaching stops on the Great North Road linking London with Edinburgh. **Parking:** There is street parking in Aberford.

Drive and Stroll

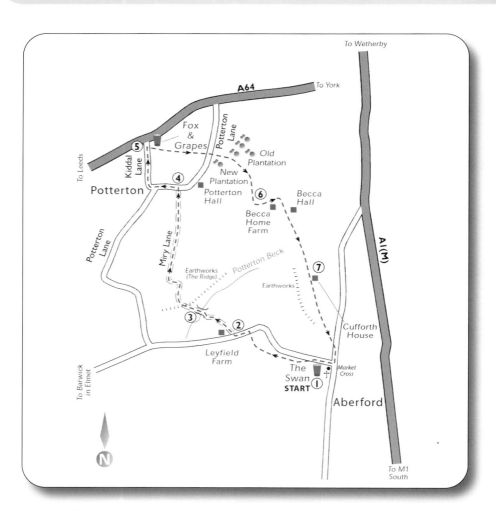

Introduction

On no account should this walk be rushed. Aberford sits beside an important network of defensive earthworks constructed by Celtic tribes, and the Romans later adapted the network for their own purposes. This route leads through these earthworks close to ancient manor houses and farms set around majestic woodlands and along well-marked bridlepaths. Walkers along these unspoiled lanes are following in the footsteps of Celts, Romans, Anglo-Saxon missionaries, Norman knights and Victorian travellers in search of antiquities. This must be regarded as a privilege.

The Swan

This is an unspoiled coaching inn and as fine as any in Britain. The old stables still surround the car park and high on a wall is a notice offering post horses for hire. Outside is a large beer garden, part of which has a glass canopy to keep off the rain. Inside, the small rooms with beamed ceilings are still retained as if waiting for wealthy coaching customers to book a private parlour.

However, you do not have to be rich to eat in this friendly place and the daily lunchtime carvery is good and substantial and the sweets are mouth-watering. The bar meals are excellent as are the dinner menu, the wine list and the beers on offer. Telephone: 0113 2813205.

THE WALK

 ①

Start from the church which has a most unusual dedication.

St Ricarius is reputed to have been a French warrior who was converted to Christianity by Irish missionaries and then went on a preaching mission to England in AD 630. Although restored in 1861, the church is still impressive.

Leave the gates of the church, turn left and pass the old market cross which may date to the 14th century or even earlier. Pass the **Swan** and turn left along the road towards **Barwick in Elmet**. Turn left along a well-marked footpath sign and follow this through a small wood. Cross a field along an obvious path to reach the **Aberford** to **Barwick in Elmet** road once more. Turn left and follow a grass verge to **Leyfield Farm**.

 ②

Turn right along a signed bridleway. The path, marked by yellow arrows, crosses **Potterton Beck** via a footbridge. Look out to the left for a distant view of **Barwick in Elmet church**. The path cuts through an obvious and substantial embankment which is known as **The Ridge**. This was part of the Brigantian defences which were breached by the Romans in a struggle lasting for two years and beginning in AD 78.

 ③

From the earthworks, the path swings right and follows the well-named **Miry Lane** which ascends gently towards **Potterton** on the right and with **Barwick in Elmet** to the left. The well-used bridlepath is lined with trees mainly of hawthorn and blackthorn and with lush fields on either side usually occupied by grazing cattle.

Miry Lane ends at the gates of

Drive and Stroll

The view from Miry Lane

Potterton Hall which is mentioned in deeds dating to the 12th century and is still privately owned. The façade of the present hall was constructed in 1720 and the rest of the residence just a little later.

 ④

Turn left at the hall and follow the quiet road. Turn right onto the more substantial **Kiddal Lane** and follow this towards the **Fox and Grapes** pub.

 ⑤

Just before this, turn right along a footpath, its line indicated by yellow arrows. The path crosses stiles and reaches **Potterton Lane**. Cross this to another footpath sign with its now familiar yellow arrow. Bear right and follow the line of a hedge until **Becca Home Farm** comes in sight.

 ⑥

Bear left around **Becca Home Farm** and then sharp right passing **Becca Hall** on the left.

Becca Hall has its origins in the 13th century when it was owned by Henry le Gramary. It was he who was granted a market charter for Aberford in 1248 and the cross mentioned at point 1 may date from this time.

 ⑦

Continue straight ahead along the substantial drive to **Becca Hall**. Follow the track back to **Aberford** passing **Cutforth House** on the left and another Celtic earthwork on the right. The track leads onto the old **Great North Road** to the north of the **Swan** and the church. Turn right to reach the **Swan**.

3 | Bramham

Bramham House

The Walk 4½ miles 🕐 2½ hours
Map: OS Explorer 289 (GR 843432)

How to get there

Bramham is signed off the A1 some 5 miles south of Wetherby, 10 miles east of Leeds and 15 miles west of York. Exit the A1 at the Bramham/Thorner junction and follow the signs to the village centre. **Parking:** There is street parking around the square and the Red Lion.

Drive and Stroll

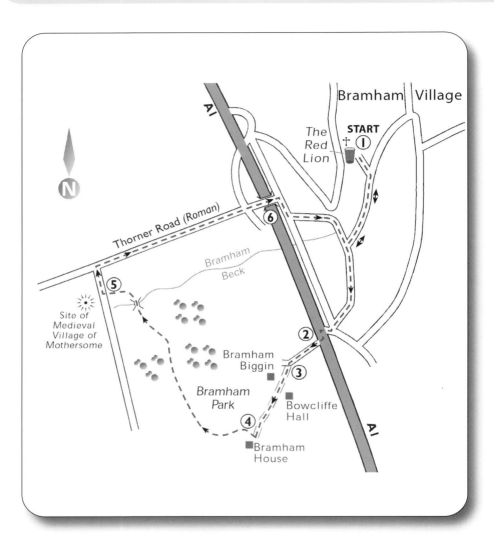

Introduction

This walk is centred around the delightful and unspoiled stone village of Bramham, which consists of 18th- and 19th-century cottages, a medieval church with a Norman tower and a solid old inn. The village is set amongst rolling countryside and is bypassed by the old Great North Road (now the A1). This walk of wonderful contrasts includes stunning scenery, one of the finest 18th-century houses in England and a deserted medieval village. Here

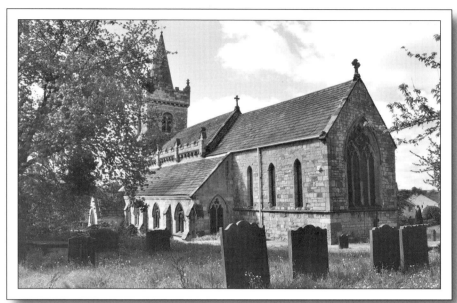

Bramham's medieval church

too are tiny, rippling streams, sizeable woodlands and a substantial Roman road. This is a route to be strolled, savoured and should never be rushed.

The Red Lion

Situated on the market square and overlooked by the war memorial, this hostelry is typical of the village – dependable and honest. The menu is varied with a local flavour, the choice of beers is wide and also with a local bias whilst the choice of wine is modest but good. Tea and coffee plus assorted sandwiches and snacks are on offer throughout the day. Telephone: 01937 843524.

THE WALK

Before setting out, explore the church which was hurriedly restored by the Victorians. The Norman tower and south door date to the

13th century, however, and make the visit worthwhile.

Bear left along the road from the **Red Lion** then turn right and approach a slip road over the **A1**.

Drive and Stroll

 ②

Cross over this and turn left along a minor road. In just over ½ mile look for a sign indicating **Bramham Park**. Turn left here towards **Bramham Biggin**. .

 ③

Follow the obvious and wide track, with **Bowcliffe Hall** away to the left.

Bowcliffe Hall dates to the 18th century and is now a business complex. To the right is another old house – Bramham Biggin – which dates to 1756.

Descend through the lush parkland

of **Bramham**. Here are open fields lined with splendid old trees. Both these features provide habitat for a rich variety of fauna and flora.

 ④

Bear right across the front of the splendid building in **Bramham Park** which is open to the public from Easter to the end of September.

Bramham Park's gardens are a joy and overlooking these is an attractive teashop and a gift shop. The house was built in the classical Queen Anne-style which is not surprising since it was the home of the Queen's Lord Chamberlain,

The Red Lion pub at Bramham

Lord Bingley. Inside are splendid portraits by Reynolds and some superb furniture and porcelain. The Bingley family still owns the house, and the stable block is in regular use. This adds to the atmosphere of this delightful place and a visit is a must.

Follow the obvious signs to the right; the path then sweeps through the rolling parkland. Pass through deciduous woodlands and over a footbridge across **Bramham Beck**. This is the haunt of the resident dipper and the summer-visiting common sandpiper.

Bear left to meet a minor road. Turn right.

On the left of the road is the site of the deserted medieval village of Mothersome. Some say that the village was deserted following improvements in agricultural techniques which meant that fewer people were needed to work the land. Others suggest that the villagers were the victims of the Black Death in the 14th century. Whatever the reason, this whole area has an agreeably haunting atmosphere.

Turn right onto **Thorner Road** which is very, very straight and obviously Roman.

At the end of the Roman road, cross over the A1 and turn first right and then left to return to **Bramham** village.

4 Wetherby

The bridge over the River Wharfe, Wetherby

The Walk 3 miles ⏱ 2 hours
Map OS Explorer 289 (GR 405479)

How to get there

Wetherby is reached from the A1 between Knaresborough in the north and Boston Spa in the south. It is set along the A659 which links Otley to the west with York to the north-east. **Parking:** Cross the road over the Wharfe Bridge at Wetherby and then immediately right into the large car park.

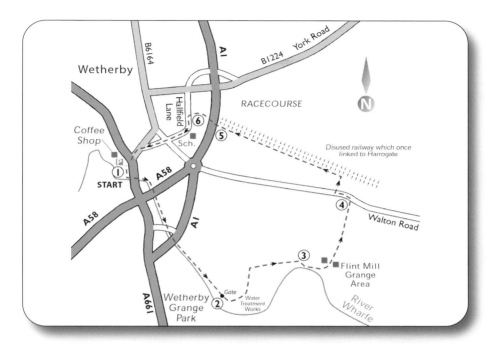

Introduction

This walk starts from a car park close to the town centre where there is a wonderful old bridge. The main feature of the town is the colonnaded shambles, which is always busy on the Thursday market day, and on the days when horse racing takes place. Although the A1 now bypasses the town, it was once a vital coaching stop on the Great North Road at which time there were more than 40 pubs and alehouses here.

The river crossing was once guarded by a castle built by the Knights Templar in the 12th century, but only the foundations now remain. The bridge is one of the most ancient spans in Yorkshire and is first mentioned as early as 1233 although it has been subject to rebuilding and widening in subsequent centuries. Close to the bridge is an old weir, which once powered a corn mill and is now maintained by a trust. The Wharfe is an unpolluted river and this is the place to enjoy wildlife throughout the year and where you might be lucky enough to spot the resident kingfisher, dipper, grey wagtail and heron.

This generous slice of history sets the scene for this pleasant stroll which follows a river and then the route of an old railway before skirting Wetherby racecourse.

Drive and Stroll

The Cottage Coffee shop

Situated close to the river and the car park, this has a spacious interior but its best feature is, without doubt, the tea garden with tables interspersed with rose bushes. The café is open daily from 10 am to 5 pm but is closed on Wednesdays. The meals are varied and cater for all tastes whilst the cream teas attract visitors from all over Yorkshire, and even beyond. Telephone: 01937 586157.

THE WALK

From the car park, walk away from the bridge and keep the river on the right. To the left are soaring cliffs. Pass underneath modern bridges which carry first the A58 and then the A1. Pass through a sturdy metal gate and follow the river on the right whilst to the left are open fields. Beyond the

Wharfe can be seen **Wetherby Grange Park**.

Pass through another gate and follow the obvious path towards the water treatment works. Bear left at the works and ascend an incline. At the summit bear sharp right and follow a pleasant grassy track to reach a slope overlooking the river.

Wetherby Shambles

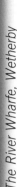
The River Wharfe, Wetherby

 ③

Cross a stile and follow a belt of trees to reach **Flint Mill Grange Farm**. Enter the road towards the farmyard, turn left and continue straight ahead.

 ④

At **Walton Road** turn left for about 80 yards and then turn right along a bridlepath and signed '**Entrance to Wetherby Racecourse**'. Around the grassy track are to be seen birds such as oystercatcher and lapwing whilst in winter redwings and starlings probe for food in the tussocks.

Pass through a gate and then turn sharp left onto the track of the disused **Church Fenton to**

Harrogate Railway. This was built in the 1840s but was closed during the 1960s. Follow the level track for around a mile. This stretch is now an excellent linear nature reserve.

 ⑤

Approach the A1 which is raised on an embankment. Pass under the road and bear slightly right and then left along a path known as **Freeman's Way**.

 ⑥

At **Hallfield Lane** turn left and pass the high school on the left. Follow the road into **Wetherby** town centre and back to the starting point.

5 | Walton

Angler's Lake

The Walk 6½ miles 🕐 3½ hours
Map OS Explorer 278 (GR 374154)

How to get there

From Wakefield look for the A638 indicating Doncaster. In around 2 miles look for a sign indicating Crofton. Follow signs to Wintersett. At the Angler's Retreat public house turn right. The Waterton Heritage Centre is reached in around ½ mile. **Parking:** Turn right into the large free car park.
Note: Squire Waterton lived at Walton Hall. Some signs indicate Walton (the estate village) whilst others refer to the famous Squire Waterton. The two names are, however, synonymous!

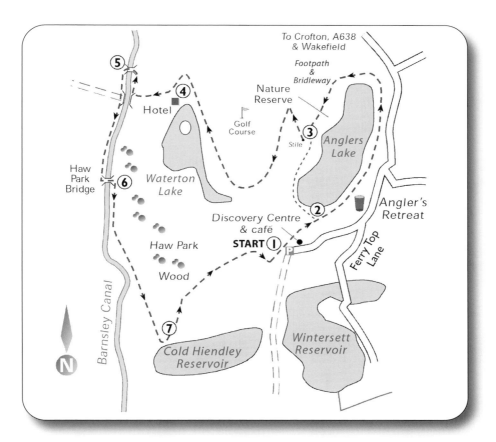

Introduction

Close to the busy city of Wakefield is this idyllic setting which, in terms of natural history and conservation, should be regarded as most important not just for local interest but internationally. Walton Hall was the home of Squire Charles Waterton (1782-1865) who set up the world's first nature reserve on his estate. This wonderfully varied stroll undulates gently around lakes, across fields, through mixed woodlands and along a canal towpath. There are plenty of places to picnic, enjoy splendid scenery and watch the fauna and flora, which would please Squire Waterton.

Squires Tearoom

Attached to the Discovery Centre is the Squires Tearoom. This is open daily

Drive and Stroll

from 10 am to 5 pm. There is a spacious interior and an outdoor patio with tables. The snacks on offer include soup and sandwiches, plus a range of filled jacket potatoes. Telephone: 01924 860282. The nearest pub is the pleasant Angler's Retreat on Ferry Top Lane.

THE WALK

Start at the **Waterton Discovery Centre** which is open free of charge but is closed on Saturdays (telephone: 01924 303980).

This is the place to celebrate the life and times of a man described by Charles Darwin as the world's first naturalist.

From the Discovery Centre follow the wide track to a fork at **Angler's Lake**.

Bear right and keep the lake on the left.

This was not a Waterton creation but he would have been proud of it. It was constructed in 1974 following the closure and landscaping of one of the largest opencast coal mining sites in Europe. There is no sign of this today and alongside the water there are benches ideal for birdwatching and picnicking. In winter this is the haunt of goldeneye, goosander and even the quite rare smew. In summer this is still the place to enjoy the

sound of the increasingly rare cuckoo and skylark.

Follow the footpath and bridleway around the lake and after just over a mile, look out for a stile in the hedge to the right.

Cross the dog-friendly stile and then over another stile leading into open fields and a golf course. The obvious track approaches Waterton Lake.

This was enlarged by Charles Waterton's father in 1790, using part of an ancient moat.

The track leads to **Walton Hall**, former home of the Watertons.

After a period of neglect, it has been developed as an upmarket hotel and renamed Waterton Park Hotel. The house was built in 1767 on the site of a previous hall dating to 1453.

Away from the hotel complex, bear right and then left along a service road to the **Barnsley Canal**.

Turn right and then left over a

Riders in the country park

bridge to reach the canal towpath.

The canal was built in 1799 and traded in coal from Barnsley in one direction and stone, and farm produce from Wakefield in the other.

Continue to **Haw Park Bridge** keeping the canal on the left. Cross the bridge and turn right.

Now keep the canal on the right and the obvious track leads through **Haw Park Wood** which was once part of the huge Don Forest, a deer hunting area in the Middle Ages.

Until 1960, the Forestry Commission managed the wood and planted large numbers of conifers to be sold for pit props.

With the closure of the mines the local Countryside Service is now replacing conifers with native hardwoods and the bird and insect life has benefited accordingly.

The track leads to **Cold Hiendley Reservoir** and beyond this **Wintersett Reservoir**.

These were built between 1854 and 1874 to provide essential water for the Barnsley Canal. From that time to the present day, the waters have provided refuge for wildlife and interest for visitors.

From Cold Hiendley the route turns sharp left and skirts **Haw Park Wood** on the left and returns to the car park.

6 | Sandal Castle, Wakefield

Sandal Castle is the start for this fine walk

The Walk 3½ miles 🕒 2 hours
Map OS Explorer 278 (GR 337182)

How to get there

Situated close to Wakefield, Sandal Castle is reached from the A61 some 2 miles south. The castle is well-signed from the A61 and reached along a network of minor roads. **Parking**: A car park has been recently constructed and there is also an excellent information centre.

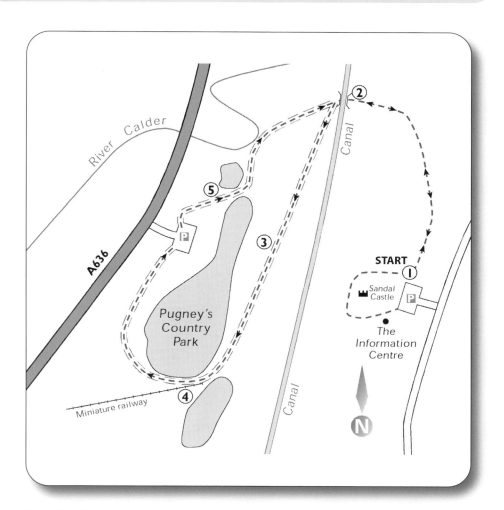

Introduction

This stroll starts from an elevated site offering panoramic views of the city of Wakefield and Pugney's Country Park. Sandal Castle played an important role in English history. Shakespeare mentions the castle in 1460 in his play Henry VI Part 3, which describes the death of the Duke of York beneath the castle walls. Shakespeare was an observant naturalist and he would have loved this stroll which is full of wildlife whatever the season. Those who want to walk through history and natural history therefore should put on their boots and enjoy a saunter around Sandal!

Drive and Stroll

Where to eat

The Information Centre has a small snack bar offering drinks and sandwiches. There is a picnic area in front of the building, and around the castle are plenty of seats ideal for enjoying a picnic. It is open on most days of the year from 10 am until 4 pm. Telephone: 01924 370211.

THE WALK

Sandal Castle was one of those which were 'slighted' on Cromwell's orders following the civil wars of the 1640s. But, in recent years, the castle has been restored and the views from the battlements are spectacular: to the north is Wakefield with the 247 ft-high cathedral spire, which is the tallest in Yorkshire, and to the west is the developing Pugney's Country Park.

Look down towards Wakefield to see a straight footpath leading through fields. These fields look spectacular in summer as the yellow rapeseed contrasts with the brown earth of the footpath, which runs through the centre of the crop.

Looking towards Pugney's Country Park

Picnicking by the castle

①

Pass through a gate and follow the footpath. Descend steeply and pass through a housing estate to an obviously signed bridge over a feeder canal from the **River Calder**.

 ②

Cross this footbridge and turn sharply left.

Look up to see Sandal Castle and enjoy the sensation of being on the site of the Battle of Wakefield, fought on the icy cold day of 30th December 1460.

 ③

To the right is the extensive lake which is an integral part of **Pugney's Country Park**.

The park is emerging from the 'flashes' created as a result of a century of coal mining. These subsidences have now flooded and provide a perfect place where wildlife-watchers, anglers and those who love watersports can pursue their hobbies.

 ④

At the miniature railway, the track sweeps to the right and provides children with a variation to their stroll and naturalists yet another chance to enjoy the varied fauna and flora. Pass through the

Drive and Stroll

The Information Centre and Coffee Shop

extensive car park, which is fast becoming the focus for a fascinating variety of amenities, including ice cream and fast food outlets, and bear right.

 ⑤

Passing a smaller 'flash' on the left, the route then sweeps left towards the meander of the **River Calder**. A right turn leads to the bridge over the feeder canal mentioned in point 2. Cross this and bear right through the houses to the field path

and return to the **Sandal Castle** car park.

A circular route is well-marked around the castle and information boards provide details of the structure which, in the last few years has been 'restored', if this is the right word to apply to a ruin. There are seats providing views down into the old moat and above to the spread of Wakefield city.

7 | Kirkstall Abbey

Kirkstall Abbey and the Abbot's House Museum

The Walk 5½ miles ⏱ 3 hours
Map: OS Explorer 288 (GR 258362)

How to get there

Situated only 2 miles north-west of Leeds city centre, Kirkstall Abbey is directly on the A65. **Parking**: The former Abbots Gatehouse is now a well-appointed museum and there is an extensive free car park here.

Drive and Stroll

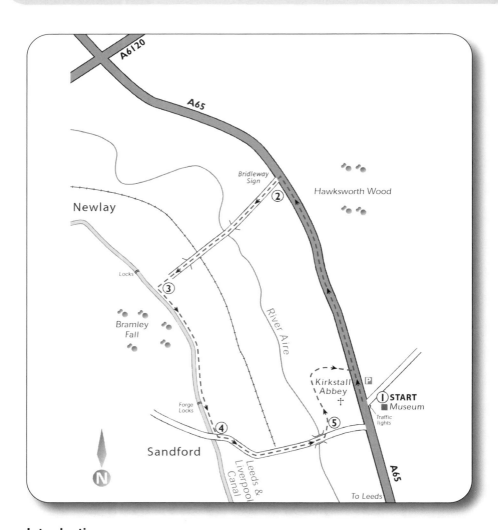

Introduction

In 2005 the wonderfully atmospheric ruins of Kirkstall Abbey were restored and a new visitor centre opened. This leads out along specially constructed and spectacular paths. Our stroll passes through ancient woodlands, over a meander of the River Aire and along the towpath of the Leeds and Liverpool Canal. The route leaves the best to the last and the abbey is acknowledged to have been one of the most spectacular and richest in the whole of England.

The Abbot's Tearooms

This is situated in the undercroft to the abbey and parts of it can be dated to the 12th century. It is a really peaceful place to enjoy a meal and the café has a drinks licence. There are all the usual dishes on offer, including ciabatta sandwiches. The ciabatta can be traced back to Roman times and made using unleavened wholegrain dough, baked in the shape of a slipper. There is also a local touch to the Yorkshire puddings, which are served with a variety of fillings. Jacket potatoes are included on the menu, and we can read a brief history of the humble spud. Apparently, when it was introduced from America by Sir Walter Raleigh in 1589, it was regarded as an expensive aphrodisiac! Beside the museum is a garden where the 'home grown' herbs and salads are supplied to the kitchen. The sweets also are often made using locally produced fruit. Telephone: 0113 2305492.

The Abbot's Tearooms

Drive and Stroll

THE WALK

 ①
Turn left from the museum.

The Abbot's House Museum (for which there is an entry fee) describes not only the history of the abbey but also displays the history of Leeds. There are reconstructed street scenes, with cobblers, blacksmiths, livery stables and the Hark to Rover pub on show.

Notice the plaque on the wall here – it indicates that our route is on the **Leeds Waterfront Heritage Trail**. Cross the A65 at the traffic lights and turn right. Follow the wide footpath alongside the A65 for about ¾ mile. Look down to the abbey grounds on the left and the ancient woodland of **Hawksworth** (meaning settlement where hawks lived) to the right of the road.

 ②
A wide public bridleway is signed. Turn left along this and follow it towards **Newlay**. Cross a bridge over the river and another over the railway. To the right along this route are the extensive **Outwood woodlands**.

 ③
Approach the **Leeds and Liverpool Canal** and turn left along the towpath. Across the canal is **Bramley Fall Woods** and also signs of an extensive and ancient quarry.

Inside the Abbot's House Museum

Stone from these quarries was used to construct Kirkstall Abbey. Stone was also taken from here to build the Martello towers in Kent during the Napoleonic wars and part of the journey to the south-east would have been along the then recently-constructed canal. A set of locks in this area is the start of the descent of the canal into the city of Leeds.

Continue to follow the towpath to **Forge Locks** and look left across the fields to see the abbey.

At **Sandford**, turn left and cross over the railway bridge and the **River Aire** once more. Again, there are spectacular views of the abbey.

Approach a war memorial and take the path on the left leading to the abbey.

The abbey was built by the Cistercians in the 12th century. It was dissolved in 1537 by Henry VIII and partly demolished. The 2005 restoration programme involved securing the sagging masonry.

From the abbey grounds and the information centre, pass through a gate which is near the traffic lights on the A65. Cross at the lights, turn left and return to the **Abbot's House Museum** and car park.

Drive and Stroll

8 Otley

The view from the Chevin down into Otley

The Walk 5 miles 🕒 Allow 3 hours to explore woodlands and the town centre
Map OS Explorer 297 (GR 204455)

How to get there

Otley is on the A660 and just off the A65 which links Ilkley with Leeds. Turn off the A660 onto the A659. A right turn from the town centre leads to the parish church of All Saints on the right. **Parking**: Turn right at the church to reach a car park on the left.

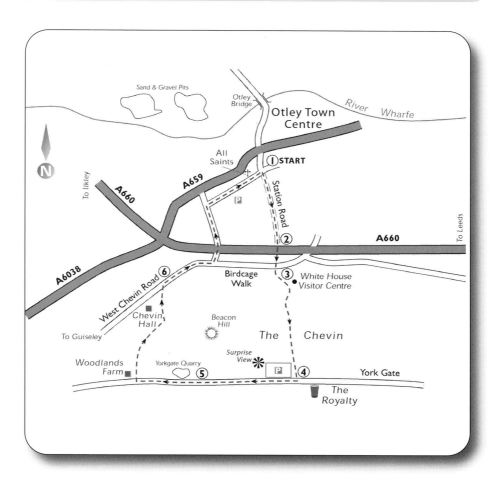

Introduction

Otley is an old unspoiled Yorkshire town away from the main tourist traps, but set close to countryside which provides inspiration for photographers and artists alike. This was certainly the case with the artist J.M.W. Turner (1775-1851), who spent time staying with the Horton-Fawkes family who lived at nearby Farnley Hall.

This walk winds its way up from the town centre through the mixed woodland to meet an old Roman road before descending back into Otley on winding footpaths abounding with wildlife. This mix of history and natural history is truly inspirational. The town itself is seen at its best during market days (Friday and Saturday).

Drive and Stroll

The Royalty

A parcel of land called the Royalty was named as such at the time of George III. In 1865 three dwelling houses were converted into an inn. It stands on the old Roman road running across the top of the Chevin and overlooking the town. The Royalty, situated close to point 4 on the walk, is open for meals from Monday to Friday, 12 noon to 2.30 pm and 5.30 pm to 9 pm. On Saturday food is served from 12 noon to 9 pm and on Sunday from 12 noon to 6 pm. There is an imaginative children's menu whilst the adult fare includes substantial portions of fish and chips and gammon steaks. The bacon and black pudding dish is excellent but vegetarians are equally well looked after. Telephone: 01943 461156.

THE WALK

The church of All Saints opposite the car park is full of treasures, including a collection of Anglo-Saxon crosses (mostly fragmented) and also a portion of an Anglo-Danish grave slab. The present church dates to the Norman period whilst close to the churchyard is one of the most fascinating memorials to be found anywhere in Britain. It commemorates the men who died whilst constructing the railway tunnel (built between 1845 and 1849) at nearby Bramhope. It is fashioned to be a copy of the tunnel entrance. The railway company decided to go 'posh' and used stone from France instead of from the local quarry. The French stone soon dissolved and in 1913 a replacement in Yorkshire stone was erected.

Before setting off on the walk, a stroll of less than ¼ mile leads down to the River Wharfe where rowing boats can be hired in the season. Between the river and the church, a plaque marks the site of the birthplace of Thomas Chippendale (1719–1779), the famous furniture maker.

①

From the church, look for **Station Road** and a footpath sign marked **Chevin**. Follow this unmade road to a bridge.

 ②

The metal bridge looks as if it should span a railway but in fact it now carries the A660 road. Cross over this bridge and turn left. In around 50 yards, look for a right turn to a footpath marked **York Gate**.

 ③

This footpath climbs steeply and to the left is the **White House Visitors Centre**.

In Otley churchyard are resident grey squirrels

Here are displays of local and natural history, and this is the place to stop and thank Major Fawkes of Farnley Hall who gave this land to the people of Otley in 1944 in memory of those who fell in the war of 1939–45. In 1989, the 700 acres (280 hectares) were designated as a nature reserve. Telephone: 01943 462454.

Continue along to **York Gate**.

York Gate is a fine example of a Roman road and links York, Tadcaster and Ilkley. Here stands the Royalty pub waiting to welcome thirsty walkers after the steep climb from Otley. Stop also to enjoy the Surprise View looking down into the town. A huge and impressive cross now dominates the summit.

Turn right along **York Gate** to a disused quarry.

From the car park of the York Gate Quarry on the right don't forget to enjoy the fact that Yorkshire stone weathered better than the French stone of the Bramhope memorial.

Just before **Woodlands Farm**, turn right onto a footpath leading back down into **Otley**.

This is a wonderful area to enjoy the wildlife, which abounds around the Chevin. Take your time as Chevin Hall is passed on the left. Look out for birds such as nuthatch, great spotted woodpecker, sparrowhawk and

Drive and Stroll

The Royalty pub on the Roman road above Otley

the occasional woodcock. Mammals to be seen include the splendidly graceful roe deer and lots of grey squirrels.

Turn right at **West Chevin Road**.

Bear left at the junction with **Birdcage Walk**. Turn right along **Burras Lane** to reach the church and the car park.

9 Dovestone Reservoir, Holmfirth

Dovestone Reservoir, with Alderman's Hill to the left

The Walk 2½ miles ⏲ Allow 2 hours
Map: OS Explorer OL1 (GR 034011)

How to get there

Dovestone Reservoir is reached from Holmfirth along the A635. From Mossley and Oldham find the Clarence pub at the junction of the A669 and the A635 and follow the sign to Holmfirth. In about one mile turn right. **Parking**: The track to the reservoir descends steeply towards a large pay and display car park (modest charges) and a toilet block.

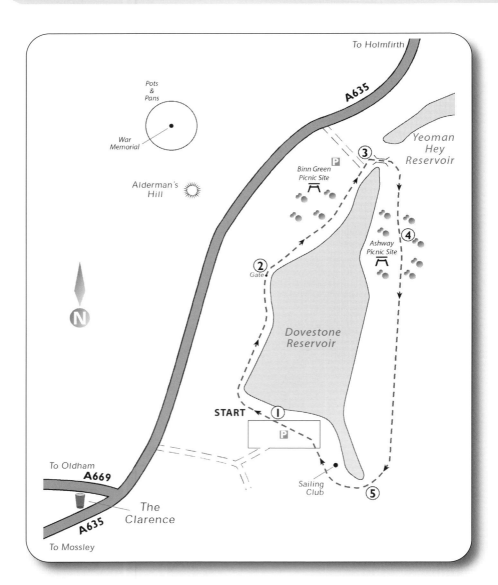

Introduction

The varied scenery of this area has regularly featured in the classic TV series, *The Last of the Summer Wine*. Here, however, is a walk which can be enjoyed on any day of the year. Apart from the obvious joys of watching colourful boats on the reservoir there are soaring views of the moorland. The route sweeps through conifer plantations, around chuckling streams and, apart from one relatively gentle climb and descent, the terrain is level. Therefore, this is the perfect walk for children and those in wheelchairs. The area is staffed by wardens and is owned by United Utilities (telephone: 01457 864187).

The Clarence

Just one mile from Dovestone, this friendly hostelry is used to walkers: a notice on the door reads 'Walkers Welcome. Muddy Boots – no problem' (there is a scraper at the door). There is an extensive outdoor area and a comfortable dining area inside. Food is served from 12 noon until 7 pm. The menu is mouth-watering: those who like traditional Yorkshire food will not be disappointed and neither will those who enjoy an international cuisine since the choice of tapas is worth travelling miles to savour. Children are welcome and have their own menu, tea and coffee are served, and the choice of hand-pulled ales is wide and should be commended. Telephone: 01457 872319.

THE WALK

**① **

From the car park, climb a set of stone steps or use the ramp and at the top of the embankment turn left.

Dovestone Reservoir is on the right. It was completed in 1967, and is one of a chain of reservoirs supplying water to Oldham and Tameside. Look down to the left to see a large paper mill which also obtains its water supply from Dovestone. The mill produces very high quality paper.

 ②

Follow the path and reach a pumping station to the right and an overflow run-off to the left. Pass through a metal gate. Turn sharp right and ascend gently through an area of conifers to the left.

The birdlife here includes jay, goldcrest, sparrowhawk and siskin. Above can be seen Alderman's Hill and Pots and Pans which is obviously named because of its shape. On top of Pots and Pans is a war memorial.

 ③

At **Binn Green** picnic site, turn sharp right over a bridge at the end of **Dovestone Reservoir**. After the bridge turn right. Away to the left is **Yeoman Hey Reservoir** built in 1880. Pass between stands of conifers.

Ashway picnic site is worth

Drive and Stroll

The Clarence pub at Greenfield

exploring. Before the construction of Dovestone Reservoir, a Victorian 'Gothic' house stood on the site. It was built as a hunting lodge by James Platt, the MP for Oldham, but he was shot dead whilst grouse hunting. During the two world wars, the house known as Ashway was used as a hospital and later it housed Italian prisoners of war. The building was considered structurally unsound in 1981 and was demolished.

(4)

Continue along the obvious path and look out over the heather and bilberry moorland to the left. Here can be seen red grouse, curlew, golden plover, raven, peregrine falcon and, in the summer months, this is the haunt of the cuckoo and the ring ouzel. Follow the undulating path to the end of the reservoir.

(5)

Sweep to the right and pass the sailing club on the right. When the boaters are out, the multi-coloured sails add an extra dimension to the joys of this beautiful walk. Continue from the sailing club and return to the car park.

10 | Saltaire

The Boathouse pub at Saltaire

The Walk 2 miles ⏱ 1½ hours but take time to travel on the Shipley Glen Tramway (see point 5)
Map: OS Explorer 288 (GR 138379)

How to get there

Situated close to both Leeds and Bradford, Saltaire is well signed from the A6038, A6037 and A650(T). Turn into the village which was constructed on a grid pattern leading to and from the wonderful old mill.
Parking: There is plenty of parking along the main streets, and the best is close to the Information Centre.

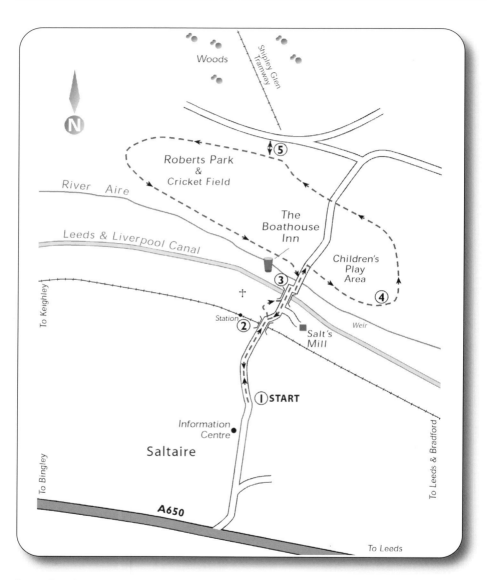

Introduction

In 2001, Saltaire was declared a World Heritage Site and is one of the most fascinating of planned industrial villages. This gentle stroll leads through the village and close to the mill, which towers over the railway, the Leeds and

Liverpool Canal and the River Aire. In addition, there is an attractive park to explore whilst a tourist tramway runs to Shipley Glen and through woodlands famous for their rich fauna and flora. The spring bluebells are renowned throughout Yorkshire.

The Boathouse

There can be very few more attractive settings to enjoy a good meal than at the Boathouse. This, as its name implies, overlooks a tranquil stretch of the River Aire. There is an outdoor area set on the bank whilst the spacious interior is the place to enjoy a bar snack or a more substantial meal. The restaurant is closed on Monday evenings but, throughout the year, speciality themed food nights reflect a worldwide cuisine and are well worth experiencing. Telephone: 01274 590408.

THE WALK

Take time to explore the compact village with its school, hospital, cottages, almshouses for the retired and meeting rooms, and then descend along the main street away from the Information Centre.

The village was developed during the 1850s when Titus Salt decided to move his Bradford Mills and associated workforce who, at the time, lived in slums, to a purpose-built complex which was named Saltaire. Eventually there was in excess of 3,000 people employed in the huge mill which had 1,200 looms weaving alpaca wool. Production only ceased in 1986 but the structure has been saved as a tourist attraction. A variety of enterprises now thrives in the area, including an organ museum and a collection of paintings by the Bradford-born artist, David Hockney.

At the railway station, take time to explore the still-operational complex which has been restored to its Victorian splendour. Nearby is the **United Reformed Church**, which includes the Salt mausoleum, and is Grade I listed. Pass the railway and then the church on the left, and follow the narrow road down to the canal bridge. Look to the right for wonderful views of the mill, the chimney of which was designed to resemble the bell tower (campanile) of St Mark's in Venice.

Pass the **Boathouse** pub on the left.

Cross the bridge over the **Aire** and take an obvious footpath immediately to the right. Follow this

Salts Mills sits on the edge of the River Aire

signed route, keeping a weir on the Aire to the right and a children's playground on the left. Pass through a delightful stretch of woodland.

In around 500 yards, turn left and continue to bear left and into

Roberts Park. This was laid out in the early 1900s to celebrate the life of Sir Titus Salt and financed by the Roberts family. To the left is a splendid cricket field.

To the right of the footpath is a sign to the **Shipley Glen Tramway**.

The Leeds and Liverpool canal at Saltaire

This funicular railway was built in the 1890s to link Saltaire with the Shipley Glen Amusement Park. The track passes through woodlands full of bluebells in spring and colourful fungi in the autumn, and is open from Easter to October and is well worth the diversion (telephone: 01274 589010).

From the tramway sign in the park, continue to follow the circular footpath and the cricket field and return to **Saltaire** via the bridges over the river, canal and railway.

11 Ilkley

The ancient bridge over the River Wharfe at Ilkley

The Walk 3 miles 🕐 Allow 3 hours to explore the church, manor house, museum and the magnificent Middleton Woods.
Map OS Explorer 297 (GR 116477)

How to get there

Ilkley is on the A65(T) road linking Skipton with Leeds. Follow the signs for the town centre. **Parking:** The large car park, situated close to the railway station and the tourist information centre, is pay and display and the impressive toilet facilities also have to be paid for. There is free parking, though, by the riverside.

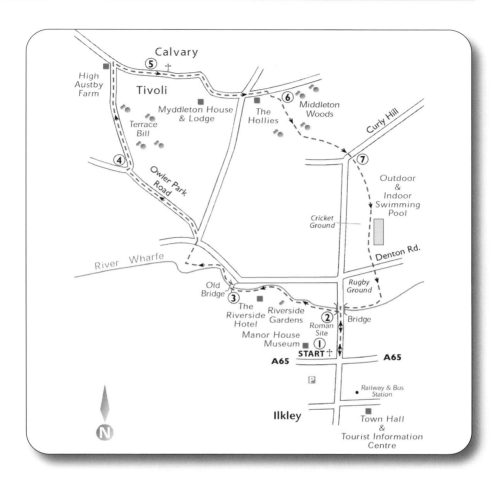

Introduction

Ilkley is a welcoming town set around an impressive meander of the River Wharfe, along which boats may be hired during the season. The town is overlooked by the famous Ilkley Moor. This is a wonderful place with or 'baht' your hat on, and this walk takes us not only up onto the old spa but alongside the Wharfe. Here are found reminders of the heyday of the Roman Empire, an ancient bridge leading to Calvary, which is a little slice of Yorkshire heaven. The route leads through ancient woodlands, on easy-to-follow footpaths and along meanders of the majestic Wharfe. Explore the old bridge and look for the masons' marks beneath the span. This is truly a stroll which can be savoured at any time of the year.

Drive and Stroll

The Riverside Hotel

Set close to the River Wharfe, this is an ideal walking base for families. The hotel is family-run and has a pleasant homely feel to it, and is child-friendly. En-suite accommodation is available and the rooms have excellent views. There is an excellent restaurant and the food is substantial and reasonably priced, with children made very welcome. Attached to the hotel on the riverside is a snack bar called the Riverside Kabin, serving meals and ice cream, with the coffee being particularly recommended. Telephone/fax: 01943 607338.

THE WALK

From the car park, head towards the station but before reaching this turn left along **Bridge Street**. Take time to explore the parish church, the manor house and the remnants of the Roman fort.

All Saints church dates back to the 13th century but was restored during the prosperous Victorian period. The pride of the place, however, are the Anglian crosses, one dating to the 9th century. They have now been brought into the church to preserve them from weathering. The Manor House museum dates from Elizabethan times and is close to the site of the Roman fort which was called Olicana. It was built to protect the ford over the River Wharfe. There is evidence that Ilkley was settled from at least the Iron Age. The museum traces this impressive history.

From the museum, follow **Brook Street** down to the modern bridge. Look out for steps on the left leading down to the attractive **Riverside Gardens**. The route then follows the gentle meander of the Wharfe on the right, whilst to the left is the children's playground and the **Riverside Hotel**.

From the Riverside Hotel find a set of steps. Ascend these and turn right over **Old Bridge**. This stone span dates to the 17th century and was a more solid replacement for a number of wooden bridges washed away by floodwaters. On the opposite side of the bridge, turn left and follow an unmade but easy-to-follow path. This reaches **Nesfield Road**. Then turn left onto **Owler Park Road**. The sign indicating a private road applies to cars but not pedestrians. The route climbs steeply and eventually appears to approach a dead end.

The Manor House Museum at Ilkley

Continue ahead, however, and follow a sign indicating **High Austby Farm**. Continue the uphill climb, with houses and fields to the left and the impressive **Terrace Gill woodland** to the right. Approach a T-junction and turn right onto a track marked **Middleton**.

Continue to the right and pass a house called **Tivoli** on the right and after about 300 yards you will see **Calvary** indicated to the left.

This is surrounded by woodland but through a gate to the left can be seen some Italianate sculptures depicting the Stations of the Cross. Enjoy this spectacle before returning to the main route. Look out to the right to see Myddleton Lodge, the Tudor spelling for a building owned by the Middletons who were Lords of the Manor. It is now a monastic retreat.

Continue to follow this track, passing **Myddleton Lodge**, and reach **Hardings Lane**.

Look for a house called **The Hollies** near which is a stile. Cross this and follow a footpath into **Middleton Woods**.

First follow a wide woodland track and, after about 200 yards, look out for a huge boulder marking a point where the path divides. Turn right and descend through the woods. Cross stone steps, a wooden footbridge over a feeder stream to the Wharfe and then go down more steps and along some boardwalks. Pass through a kissing gate.

Cross a road called **Curly Hill** and descend to **Ilkley**, passing some swimming pools (one open air) and sports fields. Cross **Denton Road** passing the rugby field on the right. Cross the road bridge and return along **Bridge Street** to the church and car park.

12 Cliffe Castle, Keighley

Cliffe Castle now houses a museum

The Walk 2 miles ⏱ 1½ hours
Map OS Explorer OL21 and 288 (GR 055420)

How to get there

Cliffe Castle is on the outskirts of Keighley off the A629 Skipton road. **Parking**: There is a free car park just off the A629. Turn right along Spring Gardens Lane and the car park, which is always open, is on the right. The museum (also free) is open daily except Mondays (other than Bank Holidays), and times are 10 am to 5 pm except Sundays when the times are 12 noon to 5 pm.

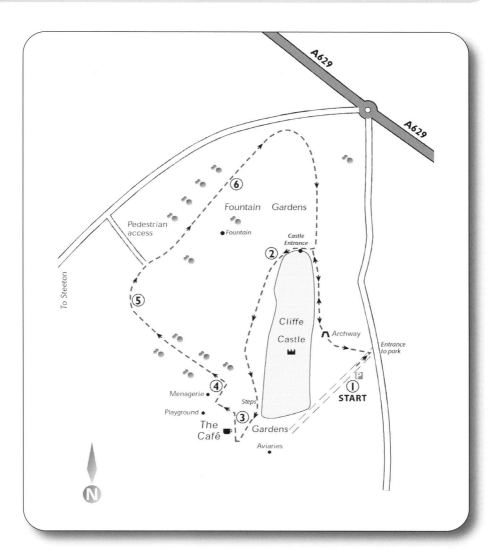

Introduction

This is an easy and undulating stroll with lots of well-positioned seats. The provision of dog bowls at the museum door is a welcome feature whilst the garden areas are colourful most of the year. The route passes through areas of mature and magnificent trees and there are panoramic views of the hills surrounding the town. Keighley developed because of textiles but the walk

Drive and Stroll

through the 300 acres of the Cliffe Castle estate feels more like a generous helping of medieval England.

Cliffe Castle Café and Museum

The clean and airy café is situated close to the aviaries and greenhouses and is surrounded by delightful gardens. The simple menu includes some interesting dishes – the home-made cottage pie and the chilli are worth a visit on their own. A good variety of coffees is served, and the children's menu is both healthy and interesting. Telephone: 01535 618231.

THE WALK

From the car park entrance turn left down the steep **Spring Gardens Lane** and turn left again after just 20 yards. Descend steeply through a rocky outcrop lined with trees.

From the castle entrance follow the well-maintained footpath around to the left.

Stop at the entrance to the castle which offers free admittance and often puts on wonderful displays, so take your time. The castle is not as old as it looks but it is no less impressive for all that. In 1828 Christopher Netherwood built Cliffe Hall in the Tudor style. Then, in 1848, the Butterfield family, who had made their fortune in textiles, bought Cliffe Hall, expanded the grounds from 20 acres to 300 acres and converted the Tudor hall into a Gothic 'castle'. In 1949 Keighley Corporation bought the castle and developed it into the town's museum. The castle attracts thousands of visitors a year, including those who just want to ramble and enjoy the rich wildlife of the grounds.

Bear left along the side of the castle. Ascend a set of stone steps.

From the steps turn right through gardens lined with seats and to the left are aviaries and greenhouses, which are open to the public. These solid structures provide colour all the year round and the heat generated inside allows native butterflies to appear early in the season and remain long after the first frost.

From the café follow the obvious footpath to the left and then turn right and descend gently.

To the left is a children's playground and ahead are large cages of domestic fowl and guinea pigs. Bear left and descend through a

The delightful teashop at Cliffe Castle

delightful area of woodland dominated by oak and horse-chestnut trees. Grey squirrels are common here and the birdlife includes great spotted woodpecker, tawny owl and sparrowhawk.

 ⑤

The route bears right and then continues straight ahead. Ignore the pedestrian access to the A6068 road to **Steeton**. Pass an old fountain on the right where there are views up to the castle. Away to the left are hills showing that **Keighley** is situated in a valley of the **River Aire**.

 ⑥

Keep following the circular path around the park passing another large fountain to the right and with wonderful old trees to the left. The route then gradually swings right and returns to the **Cliffe Castle** entrance and beyond this to the car park.

13

Harden Beck

The splendid Malt Shovel at Ilkley

The Walk 2½ miles ⏱ 1½ hours
Map OS Explorer 288 (GR 089379)

How to get there

From Keighley on the A650(T), approach the outskirts of Bingley. To the left is the fire station opposite which is a set of traffic lights. The huge parish church is to the right. Turn right at these traffic lights and cross the bridge over the River Aire. Follow the B6429 to Harden. At Harden turn left along a minor road signed Wilsden. Descend towards a bridge over Harden Beck. **Parking**: There is roadside parking just before the bridge. Beyond the bridge is the Malt Shovel.

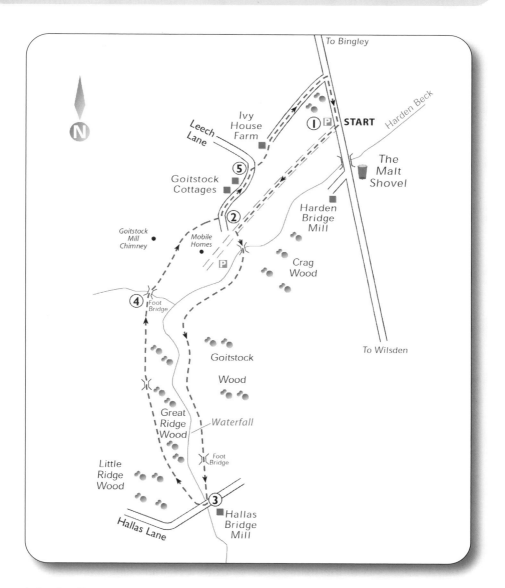

Introduction

This splendidly rural stroll on the outskirts of the city of Bradford is brim-full of interesting wildlife and contrasting scenery. Part of the walk follows a delightful stream along which are some beautiful waterfalls. There is occasional evidence to show that the beck flirted with the Industrial Revolution but it caused little damage and provides the modern walker with a gentle feeling of nostalgia. Whatever the time of year this circuit will never disappoint.

The Malt Shovel

Once a 16th-century farmhouse, the Malt Shovel has served as a coaching house, courthouse and a prison. Hanging sessions were once held here, and those to be executed were taken onto Harden Moor. Many of those condemned were 'whittlers' – those who snipped pieces off coins and forged their own coins (see also walk 18, page 85). What is now the 'snug' of the inn was the cell, and the bar was once the courtroom. There is also a large, attractive beer garden to the side and rear of the pub and, at the beer garden entrance, there is a horse trough (where your horse may slake its thirst). The menu is varied, and the roast beef dinners are as good as any in the country. The soup and sandwiches attract many walkers, and vegetarians and children are very well catered for. Telephone: 01535 272357.

THE WALK

①

From the parking area, find a wide track signed to a caravan park. Turn right and keep **Harden Beck** on the left.

The stream is fringed by trees and is a delight at all times but especially in late autumn and winter when the leaves have fallen. Here are resident dippers and grey wagtails. To the left can be seen Harden Bridge Mill which was one of many mills built around the Bradford countryside and was once powered by water. This old mill is now a print works.

Continue ahead and approach a caravan site on the right with its private car park on the left.

②

The path leads to a bridge over the beck. Cross this and turn right. Pass a bungalow on the left and the beck is now on the right. Pass through **Goitstock Wood** with its rich and seasonally varied fauna and flora. At this point the track becomes rough, and undulating and solid handrails have been provided. This steep area leads to two splendid waterfalls. Cross a footbridge and approach **Hallas Bridge**. Here is another old mill which has recently been tastefully converted to residential use.

③

At **Hallas Lane** turn very sharp right

The delightful waterfall by Goitstock Wood

along a footpath which passes through **Little Ridge** and **Great Ridge Woods**. This area is popular with naturalists and here can be found the resident jay, the tawny owl, treecreepers and the occasional nuthatch. Pass through three substantial stiles.

 ④

Cross a metal footbridge. Keep a well-maintained dry stone wall to the right. Look out for the chimney

of **Goitstock Mill**. The mill itself has gone but its chimney is a reminder of a once industrial age. The footpath bears gently right.

 ⑤

Meet **Leech Lane** and, as this turns left, follow the footpath straight ahead. Pass **Ivy House Farm** on the left and continue to meet the **Wilsden Road**. Turn right to the starting point and the **Malt Shovel**.

14

Shibden Hall

Shibden Hall was built in the 15th century

The Walk 5½ miles 🕐 2½ hours
Map OS Landranger 104 (GR 108259)

How to get there

Although almost in the centre of Halifax, Shibden Hall and Country Park was once in the heart of a fertile valley. It is now clearly signed from Halifax but surrounded by a network of major roads including the A58 linking Rochdale with Leeds and also nearby is the A647. **Parking**: Shibden Hall is well-signed from both the A58 and A647; a narrow minor road leads to the hall where there are several free car parks.

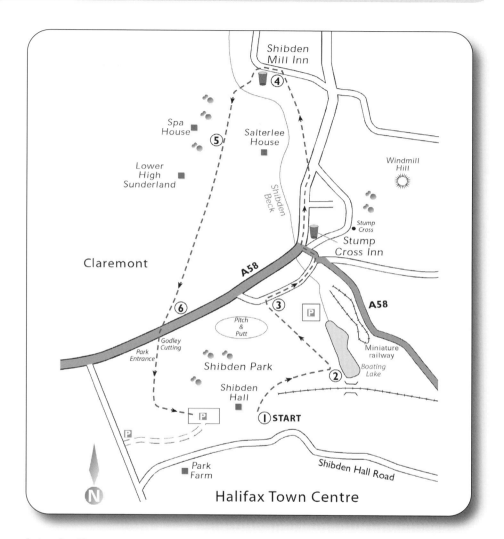

Introduction

Those who think that Halifax is just a mucky old wool town generated by the Industrial Revolution should think again! This walk follows an ancient track linking Lancashire and Yorkshire; wanders through 90 acres (36 hectares) of luxuriant parkland, passes a half-timbered manor dating to around 1420 and then travels along the banks of Shibden Brook. The word Shibden is derived from 'the valley of the sheep' and the area certainly made its fortune

Drive and Stroll

from wool. In 2004 a Heritage Lottery Grant of £3.7 million was awarded as part of a £6 million project to restore the Shibden Estate. This has involved the creation of a network of new and well-marked footpaths through the area.

Despite flirting with the modern town of Halifax, this walk is an example of West Yorkshire countryside at its very best.

The Café, Shibden Hall

There are several hostelries in the area but, at the hall, there is an excellent café which is open every day. There is a children's menu, with the accent on wholesome food. Here is the place for nourishing soup, hot sandwiches, including corned beef and pickles, and the famous toasted crumpet! This is also the place to get one of the best cups of tea in Yorkshire! For the warmer days, there is a good outdoor area, which takes the pressure off the limited space within. Telephone: 01422 352246.

THE WALK

From **Shibden Hall**, follow the obvious track down to the **boating lake**.

It is thought that Emily Brontë used Shibden Hall as her model for Thrushcross Grange in her only novel, Wuthering Heights, *published in 1847. And, if you read her description of Thrushcross Grange after visiting Shibden, you will be in no doubt and this was used in the 1991 version of the film* Wuthering Heights *starring Ralph Fiennes as Heathcliffe and Juliette Binoche as Cathy.*

Just four families, the Oates, Saviles, Waterhouses and especially the Listers, have lived at the hall since 1420, and this continuity could possibly be one of the

reasons why it has survived so well.

Since 1934 the hall has been a museum run by the local council. Although not particularly famous for its gardens, Shibden does have some fine examples of teasel plants. The sharp bristles of their seed heads made them useful for brushing woollen cloth to raise the knap, in particular it was employed in the production of the cloth used for the first commercial billiard tables.

The lake, park and children's playground are popular throughout the year. A good romp plus feeding the wildfowl especially in winter makes this walk ever popular with families.

Ascend a track (**Old Godley Lane**) which meets the busy A58.

Shibden Park is home to some fine teasel plants

 ③

Turn left onto **Staups Lane** passing the **Stump Cross Inn** to the right. Continue to ascend the lane which soon becomes cobbled. At the end of the paving at **Shibden Dale** pass through a gate on the left and follow a field path and then a track to the left and descend to the **Shibden Mill Inn**. This is a fine conversion of the old mill and is an enjoyable place to eat a meal.

 ④

At the end of the hotel car park follow an obvious track and cross a footbridge over **Shibden Beck**.

Shibden Mill was water powered (by Shibden Beck) and was an important site during the beginning of the Industrial Revolution.

 ⑤

Pass **Spa House** on the right. This is the only tangible reminder of Halifax's ambition to become a spa town to rival Ilkley, Knaresborough and especially Harrogate. Pass along a series of walled tracks, between the hamlets of **Claremont** and **Shibden Fold**. Pass through **Godley Cutting**.

 ⑥

Pass over the A58 and clearly seen is the **Shibden Park** entrance. Pass the pitch-and-putt course on the left and descend the obvious track back down to the Hall.

15 | Scammonden Water

Nont Sarah's at Scammonden

The Walk 3 miles ⏱2 hours
Map OS Explorer 288 (GR 055164)

How to get there

Scammonden can be seen from the M62 motorway. The easiest way to reach the reservoir is to turn off at exit number 23 and follow the A640 to Outlane. Continue along the A640 and follow the brown sign to the right indicating Scammonden Sailing Club. Nont Sarah's Inn is along the A640 about one mile from Scammonden Water. **Parking**: Do not enter the sailing club to the left but continue straight ahead to the large car park overlooking the water.

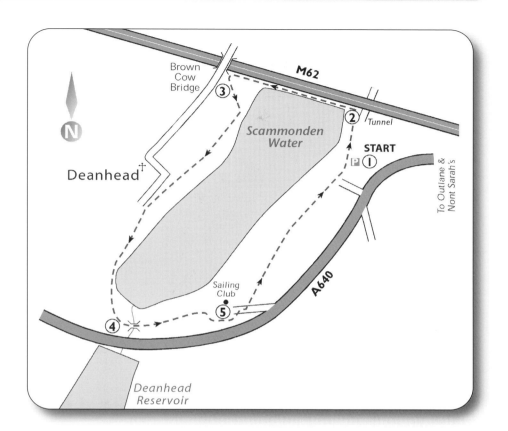

Introduction

This walk has to be unique not only in Yorkshire but in the world! Here it is possible to enjoy the glory of a transatlantic liner, the sight of the highest motorway in Britain, and a relatively recently-built reservoir which has quickly been colonised by wildlife. The route passes pretty feeder streams, an ancient hamlet, and colourful boats add even more to the atmosphere. The walk crosses land which was once farmed by the Vikings, so here is the best of both worlds – ancient and modern – blended to perfection.

Nont Sarah's Inn

Apart from excellent food, this hostelry has history in abundance. Its name is said to derive from a local lad who borrowed money from his aunt to

Drive and Stroll

establish a pub in Lancashire. This did well, so he bought another hostelry at Scammonden and named it 'Nont Sarah's', in gratitude to his benefactress. Some say that the old lass still visits on occasions to see how well her investment is faring! She would be pleased to know that it is doing very well because, if you are looking for a wonderful place to eat, this is it. The famous old ocean liner, the *Mauritania*, which was built in 1906, was broken up in 1935 and timber from her staterooms was bought and taken to Nont Sarah's. It was used in the construction of a sun lounge in the shape of a ship's bridge. Opened in 1939, it is thought to be the first 'themed pub' to be opened in Britain. Food is served daily and there are excellent facilities. The menu is truly international and served in a manner which would not disappoint passengers on the *Mauritania*. Portions are large but there is the sensible option of being able to order a smaller one. Telephone: 01484 842848.

THE WALK

①

From the car park pass a toilet block on the left and go over a stile. After about 100 yards, the footpath starts to wind to the left and descends steeply towards the reservoir.

Turn right to reach a pier-like structure. To the right is a plaque on a wall indicating that the reservoir was declared open by Queen Elizabeth in October 1971. Look straight ahead to see a tunnel under the M62 motorway. At one time the footpath round the reservoir passed through this tunnel but recently a new footpath has been opened. Ascend a steep grassy track to reach a substantial footpath. Turn left and follow this track, which is also a cycle way and is on top of the reservoir dam embankment.

Turn left but first look ahead to see the **Brown Cow Bridge** (named after a restaurant of the same name) over the M62. This soars 120 feet above the motorway and has a span of 410 feet. The path descends to the reservoir and turns right keeping the water on the left. High to the right is the church at the hamlet of **Deanhead**. This was built in 1863 to replace an earlier building of 1615.

A stream leads out of **Scammonden Water** and flows on to **Deanhead Reservoir**. The route sweeps left here and passes over two wooden footbridges. This is the place to see the Scammonden valley at its best. It is said that Scamden was a Norseman who settled hereabouts.

Scammonden Water

From the footbridges turn sharp left but look to the right towards the small Deanhead reservoir. This was built in 1832 to provide water to power the textile mills.

 ⑤

Turn right and then left to see the **Activity Centre and Sailing Club**.

Cross the access road to the sailing club and take time to watch not only the colourful boats but also the wildfowl which share the water with them. From the sailing club bear left and then right. Follow the steep track back to the car park but in the summer take time to enjoy the flowers which include a number of orchid species.

16 | Blackmoorfoot

Blackmoorfoot Reservoir

The Walk 2½ miles 🕑 2 hours
Map OS Explorer 288 (GR 105128)

How to get there

From Oldham follow the A62 towards Huddersfield. At Slaithwaite take the B6109 towards Meltham. After around 2 miles, turn left and ascend a minor road to Blackmoorfoot. Pass the Bulls Head pub on the left. Carry straight ahead into a dip in the road and ascend once more. At a bus turning point on the right, turn sharp right onto a narrow road and, after ½ mile, turn right along a cul-de-sac signed Reservoir Side Road. **Parking**: There is plenty of parking along this quiet road. On the opposite side of the road from the Bulls Head is a large car park for patrons.

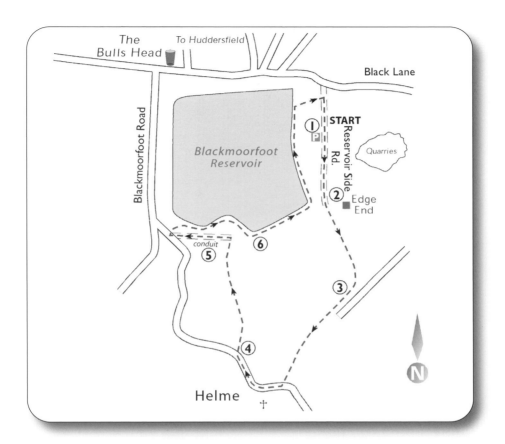

Introduction

Blackmoorfoot is regarded as a premier site for bird watching in Yorkshire, especially those in search of rare gulls. The walk leads through wonderful woodlands and the hauntingly beautiful hamlet of Helme. There are signs that the area flirted with the Industrial Revolution but the countryside hereabouts is quite unspoiled. Walking by these woodlands and watersides is a delight not to be missed.

The Bulls Head, Blackmoorfoot

A wide choice of beers is to be found at the Bulls Head, and there is also a good selection of teas and coffees. Children are made welcome, and there is a choice of menu for those with large or small appetites. The mixed grill is excellent value, the steaks are well recommended, and there are plenty of vegetarian options.

With the excellent decor and the unusual dining area set along a gallery, the Bulls Head is a delightful place to enjoy a meal. Telephone: 01484 842713.

THE WALK

From the car park, follow the wide track passing old quarries on the left and the reservoir, seen through trees and rhododendrons, to the right. The track meets a few houses at **Edge End**.

At **Edge End** continue straight ahead along a very obvious and well-signed bridleway. Descend the track. This can be muddy after rain but perhaps this should be seen as a welcome feature since the rain also provides the damp conditions suitable for the feeding grounds of lapwings.

The bridleway approaches a very minor road but do not cross this. Turn right and follow a sign to **Helme**. Cross a footbridge over a tiny stream and approach a minor road. Turn right into the hamlet of **Helme**.

This delightfully unspoiled settlement has several three-storeyed cottages, which were occupied at one time by handloom weavers, with the top floor allowing them to make the most of every minute of daylight. The church looks to be 15th-century Gothic but in fact it dates only to 1859. It was built in memory of Charles Brooke who died at the age of just 27. He was a member of the family world famous for its production of top-grade sewing cotton.

Follow the only road through **Helme** and look for an obvious footpath to the right. Pass through a gate and then into a wood. This is the haunt of woodcock which is resident here, and in winter the flocks of chaffinches are occasionally joined by the much rarer brambling.

The wood climbs steeply to meet a conduit associated with the reservoir. Turn left and follow the line of this conduit to the road from **Helme**. Join this road for only a few yards before turning sharp right. The conduit is now on the right and **Blackmoorfoot reservoir** is to the left. Continue to follow the obvious track around the reservoir.

Weavers' cottages at Helme

 ⑥

Turn left around the reservoir shoreline along which are situated a number of seats ideal for picnicking and bird watching.

Blackmoorfoot was built in the 1870s to supply water to Huddersfield at a time when the woollen industry, and its associated population, was increasing rapidly. The construction of reservoirs has proved extremely beneficial to wildfowl. Beforehand, they needed to journey over desolate areas of moorland, but human enterprise has provided them with the equivalent of our motorway services.

Continue to follow the wide reservoir track and return to the car on the right of **Reservoir Side Road**.

17 | Haworth

A footbridge close to the Brontë Falls

The Walk 6 miles ⏱ 3 hours
Map OS Explorer OL21 (GR 027372)

How to get there

Haworth is reached by turning off the A629 road linking Halifax with Keighley. There is a station on the Keighley and Worth Valley Steam Railway. From the railway station follow North Street uphill and follow the signs for the Brontë parsonage museum. **Parking**: There is a large pay and display car park here.

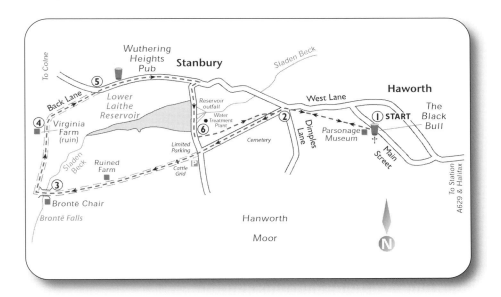

Introduction

This bright and breezy walk is sure to inspire those who love the novels of the Brontë sisters. And, indeed, the sisters loved this stroll which leads from the village to the clear streams, tumbling waterfalls and panoramic views of the valley of the River Worth. Haworth abounds with teashops, cafés and welcoming pubs along the steep and cobbled Main Street which the Brontë girls would still recognise. Please remember that this walk goes through sheep country, so dogs should be kept on a lead.

The Black Bull

Dating to the 18th century, this sturdy, square building which dominates the main street will be forever associated with Branwell Brontë (1817–1848) who drank (to excess) here: the Masonic lodge met at the Black Bull and Branwell was its secretary. Today, the Black Bull offers, amongst other things, good food, ales, wines, tea and coffee. There is a substantial menu, and it is worth sampling the home-roasted ham or the lamb in mint gravy. There is a children's menu and good vegetarian options. The place has a cosy atmosphere and, although it is now open-plan, it is easy to envisage the original design as the beams have been retained. It is just the place to build up strength following a ramble around the Brontë Falls. Telephone: 01535 642249.

Drive and Stroll

THE WALK

Before setting out on the walk, it is worth spending some time exploring the village (there is a Tourist Information Centre near the Black Bull). The church is also worth a visit. Mr Wade was the successor to Patrick Brontë (father to the famous sisters and brother Branwell) as vicar here and rebuilt and enlarged the church of St Michael and All Angels in the 1880s. The Parsonage is now a museum run by the Brontë Society and the interior is much as the Brontës would have remembered it. Here Emily (1818–1848) wrote Wuthering Heights, *Charlotte (1816–1855) penned* Jane Eyre *and Anne (1820–1849) composed* The Tenant of Wildfell Hall.

From the **Brontë Parsonage Museum** follow a narrowing footpath and then cross a field by way of a paved path. Pass through a stile.

Veer left onto **Cemetery Road** and continue for just over ½ mile to reach a T-junction. Continue straight ahead along a rough track. To the right is **Lower Laithe Reservoir**.

The reservoir was built in the 1870s and would not have

been known to the Brontës. It has, however, settled into the landscape and is a refuge for wildfowl, especially in the winter.

Go through a stile and over a cattle grid and follow the obvious track over moorland for about 1½ miles, passing a ruined farm to the right. This is now part of the **Millennium Way**.

Descend a steep causeway and approach the footbridge over **Sladen Beck** and look to the left for two Brontë associations. Here is a rock shaped like a chair and it is said that Emily spent time sitting on this stone whilst composing her narratives. The **Brontë Falls** are more of a cascade than a full-blown waterfall but they look and sound spectacular, especially after rain. Cross the bridge and turn right. Ascend a steep rough track among substantial boulders and then go through a gap in a stone wall where there is a gate. (Remember that this is sheep country so please close the gate.) The path now ascends steeply to the right via steps and a rocky path. At the top of the rise bear gently to the left close to the ruins of **Virginia Farm**.

Bear right, cross a field and over a ladder stile. Cross another field and through a stile which leads

Main Street in Haworth

The Black Bull in Haworth

along **Back Lane**. Follow this lane to the junction with the minor road linking **Haworth** with **Colne**.

 (5)

Turn right through the village of **Stanbury**, with its pub appropriately called 'Wuthering Heights'. Turn right along the substantial road over the embankment of the **Lower Laithe reservoir**.

 (6)

At the end of the embankment turn sharp left along a footpath passing the Water Treatment Works on the left. A short distance beyond this the path forks. Take the right fork and ascend to meet **Cemetery Road**. Follow a well-worn track and then right across **West Lane**. In less than 100 yards pass through a stile turn left and return to the starting point.

18 | Heptonstall and Hebden Bridge

Hebden Bridge

The Walk 3 miles ⏱ 2½ hours
Map: OS Landranger 103 (GR 978284)

How to get there

Hebden Bridge lies astride the A646 between Halifax and Todmorden, and Heptonstall is situated off a minor road from Hebden Bridge to Burnley. From the Halifax direction there is no right turn at traffic lights to reach the minor road, so continue towards Todmorden for just under ¼ mile to reach a turning circle on the left. Turn around at this point and return to the traffic lights. Turn left and climb a steep hill. In around 1 mile, turn left into Heptonstall. **Parking**: There is extensive free parking indicated clearly to the left at the Social Centre from which this walk begins.

Drive and Stroll

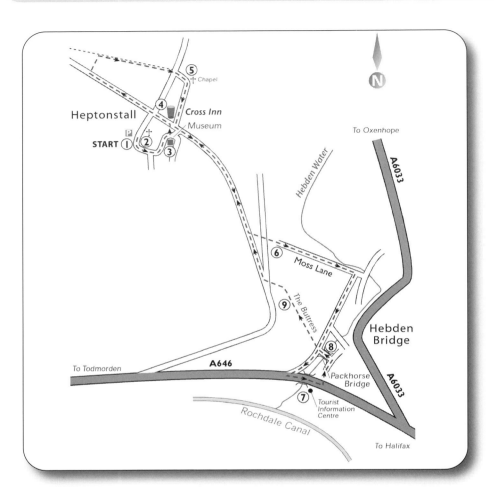

Introduction

This walk follows an undulating route along the magnificent dale of the river Hebden rich in wildlife and even richer in industrial archaeology. Packhorses carried the wool to be processed by handloom weavers in Heptonstall and the village has many weavers' cottages and also a Cloth Hall which is now a private dwelling. Down in Hebden Bridge, there are signs of the early days of the Industrial Revolution and also one of the finest packhorse bridges to be found anywhere in England. This varied and ever-changing stroll also passes the Rochdale Canal and the river named Hebden Water from which the bridge takes its name.

The Cross Inn on Towngate

This 18th-century hostelry was built, as its name implies, at a crossroads of ancient highways. In the modern context this does not seem to make much sense but the roads in question are at a junction of what, in the 18th century, were vital cross-Pennine connections linked by packhorse trails. The Cross Inn serves snacks daily, as well as substantial meals using mainly local produce of high quality. There are beers from the Timothy Taylor brewery and a wide selection of coffees. Telephone: 01422 843833.

THE WALK

From the **Social Centre** cross the road and follow a substantial track through houses on the right and with open fields to the left. Approach the large church tower and follow the circular track around the churchyard.

This is not actually one church but two - a real touch of ancient and modern. The ruins are of the church of St Thomas à Becket dating to 1260 and the path around it and its substantial Victorian replacement are lined with gravestones. One grave, which is not inscribed, is that of David Hartley described as a coiner who was buried in 1770. He was hanged for 'coining' which means that he took the coin of the realm and cut pieces from it, which he melted down to produce counterfeit coins. His gang was rounded up and Hartley himself paid the price. A plaque in the old church precincts marks the location of his grave.

From the churches return to the only gate and turn sharp left. Among a row of old cottages is the **Heptonstall Grammar School**.

Heptonstall Grammar School is now a museum (usually open at weekends) and describes the history of the village. Founded in 1642, the school was rebuilt in 1772 and closed in 1889. Telephone: 01422 843738.

Follow the narrow paved track beneath the **Great North Gate** to meet the main road through the village.

At the **Cross Inn**, turn left and follow the steep and narrow road up through **Heptonstall** with its 18th-century weavers' cottages to right and left and the village pump on the left, just off **Silver Street**. After about ¼ mile, look for a sign to the right indicating an ancient packhorse track. Turn right and descend the paved track back into the village.

Drive and Stroll

The Methodist chapel at Heptonstall

⑤

This leads to the historic **Wesleyan chapel**.

This is called the Heptonstall Octagon and was completed in 1764. It is still used for worship and is therefore the oldest Wesleyan chapel in the world which is still functioning. Its octagonal shape is said to be designed so that the devil had no corners in which he could hide!

From the chapel, follow the cobbled road to the village and approach the **Cross Inn** on the right. Turn left and descend the steep road to the minor road linking **Hebden Bridge** and **Burnley**. Turn right for around 100 yards.

⑥

Just before the 30 mph road sign, look for a left turn at **Lee Mount**. Descend the steep track along **Moss Lane** to **Hebden Bridge**. Turn sharp right along a narrow road. This leads to the main **A646** linking **Todmorden** with **Halifax**. Turn left and follow the main street in the direction of Halifax. After about 400 yards look for the new **Information Centre** on the right.

⑦

The Information Centre is situated next to the wharf of the **Rochdale Canal**.

The canal opened in 1804 and runs from the centre of Manchester to Sowerby Bridge a distance of around 30 miles. The Rochdale Canal Society and local councils have combined to restore the canal and one of its major tourist attractions is around the Hebden Bridge wharf.

From the wharf retrace the route for about 200 yards to reach a street to the right. After another 200 yards, pass a pay-and-display car park on the left which is close to the packhorse bridge.

Turn left and cross the substantial pedestrianised packhorse bridge which spans the often fast-moving **Hebden Water** and which dates to 1510. Look for the **Hole in the Wall pub** to the right whilst straight ahead is a thoroughfare known as **Old Gate**. A sign indicates 'Heptonstall (½ mile)'. Climb the cobbled causeway called the **Buttress** which is a wonderfully preserved packhorse route. There are plenty of places to stop and admire the view down to **Hebden Bridge** which developed when industry moved from handloom weaving in the hillside village to water-powered factories down in the valley.

Continue to ascend the **Buttress** until the **Burnley** to **Hebden Bridge** road is reached. Turn left and after around 100 yards turn sharp right back into **Heptonstall**. The visitors' car park is signed to the left – ascend the road to reach the starting point.

Drive and Stroll

19 | Lumbutts

Some of the spectacular countryside around Lumbutts

The Walk 3 miles 🕐 2 hours
Map OS Explorer OL21 (GR 955235)

How to get there

From the A646 Hebden Bridge to Todmorden road, find a sign for Mankinholes and Lumbutts. Cross the River Calder and the Rochdale Canal. Bear right and then follow a narrow and winding bend which climbs steeply. Towards the summit bear sharp right still following the signs to Lumbutts and Mankinholes. Just before the hamlet of Lumbutts is the Shepherd's Rest on the left. Descend into Lumbutts. **Parking**: There is roadside parking in Lumbutts.

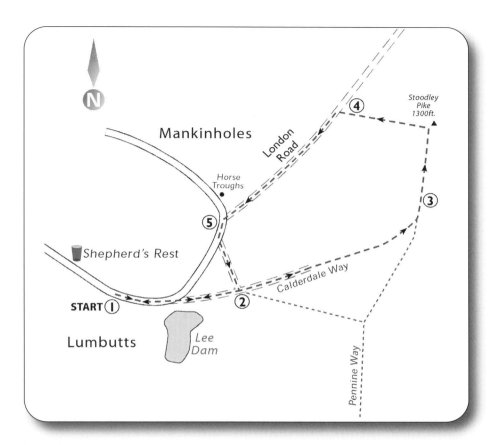

Introduction

This undulating walk is sure to delight the historian, the industrial archaeologist, and the naturalist, not to mention those who just want to walk in spectacular countryside. There are open views upwards to an historic monument and below to the Yorkshire Calder Valley, with the Rochdale Canal running through it, together with a main road parallel to the railway, and the meandering River Calder also visible.

The Shepherd's Rest Inn, Lumbutts

This building began life as a farmhouse and in 1846 it was established as an agricultural museum. This was so popular that the museum was moved to the more prosperous town of Accrington in Lancashire in 1850. William

Drive and Stroll

Butterworth then purchased the building and its stables which still stand. In 1859 he obtained a beer licence and named the place the Shepherd's Rest Inn.

Food is served every evening but the pub is closed Monday and Tuesday lunchtimes (open again in the evenings). The food here is excellent and the Sunday roasts are famous. All tastes are catered for but the Bury black pudding starter served with mustard is deservedly popular, as is the steak and ale pie. The vegetarian options are mouth-watering, especially mushroom stroganoff and the spinach and ricotta dish. With the excellent decor and the unusual dining area set along a gallery, the Shepherd's Rest Inn is a delightful place to enjoy a meal. Telephone: 01484 842713.

THE WALK

Lumbutts is dominated by an unusual chimney-like structure below which is a mill lodge always popular with water birds and a hunting ground for swallows and swifts during the summer. The tower-like structure is not actually a chimney but the housing for three overshot waterwheels, one on top of another and fed by a unique system of syphons. These are a source of wonder to industrial archaeologists. The complex is now the base for the Lumbutts Activity Centre which runs hostel accommodation for those enjoying outdoor activities.

Follow the road towards **Mankinholes** for about 200 yards and turn right onto a footpath and bridleway which is part of the **Calderdale Way**. This track and many others in the area were once packhorse routes and the flat and well-worn causeway stones are still very evident. To the left of this track are splendid views up to **Stoodley Pike**.

Climb gently to meet the junction with the **Pennine Way**, which comes in from the right. Continue straight ahead and climb steeply along the Pennine Way. The path then bears left.

The path climbs up to the summit of the 1,300-ft **Stoodley Pike**.

The Pike was built in 1814 to celebrate the French surrender of Paris and Napoleon's exile to Elba. Before the monument was completed, however, 'Old Boney' escaped and literally met his Waterloo in 1815. This time he was sent to St Helena, from which there was no escape. The views from 120-ft tower's observation platform are spectacular.

The famous horse troughs in Mankinholes

Drive and Stroll

The descent from the Pike should be taken slowly, and perhaps be interrupted by a leisurely picnic in order to have time to appreciate how 'industry' crept down from the hills and into the heart of the Calder valley. Still visible in the area are the handloom weavers' cottages and farms (including the Shepherd's Rest) linked by old packhorse routes. These weavers' cottages were superseded first by water-powered and then by steam-driven mills. The latter mills were so productive that they demanded more efficient transport systems. Spread out below is the ribbon-like Rochdale Canal, a 33-mile cut slicing through the Pennines between Manchester and Sowerby Bridge. In 2004 the final restoration of the canal was completed.

The single track down from the **Pike** meets the much wider track known as **London Road**. This was indeed once the main road in the days of the packhorse. Turn left and follow **London Road** towards **Mankinholes**.

Turn left into **Mankinholes** hamlet. Look to the right to see a long line of horse troughs. These allowed packhorses to drink without the driver having to remove any harnesses or loads. Turn left at the end of **Mankinholes** and ascend gently to the meeting of the **Calderdale Way** and the **Pennine Way**. Pass through a gate and turn right. Descend the gentle causeway back to **Lumbutts**.

20 | Warland

The route through Warland Gate End

The Walk 5½ miles ⏱ 3 hours
Map: OS Explorer OL21 (GR 944201)

How to get there

The walk starts at a large lay-by next to the Bird i' th' Hand pub which is directly on the A6033 road between Todmorden and Littleborough.
Parking: In the lay-by.

Drive and Stroll

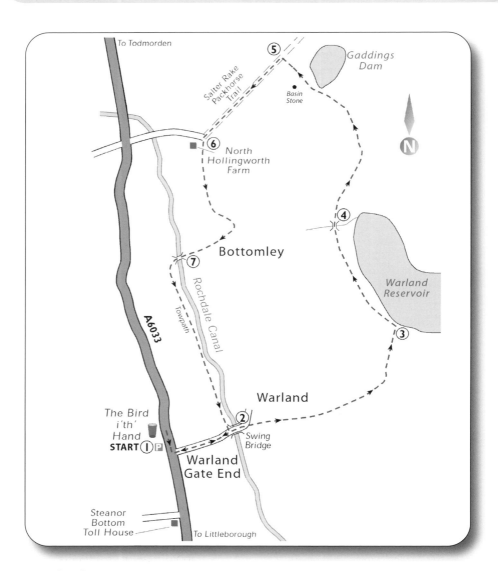

To Todmorden

⑤

Gaddings Dam

Salter Rake Packhorse Trail

Basin Stone

N

⑥ North Hollingworth Farm

④

Bottomley

Warland Reservoir

⑦

Rochdale Canal

Towpath

A6033

③

Warland

The Bird i'th' Hand
START ①🅿

②

Swing Bridge

Warland Gate End

Steanor Bottom Toll House

To Littleborough

Introduction

This is a borderlands walk where Yorkshire and East Lancashire meet. Here is moorland majesty, a reservoir ramble, an ancient packhorse track and the walk concludes along a stretch of the recently restored Rochdale canal. This restoration was completed in 2004 and has stimulated the improvement of footpaths, including clear indication arrows. The ascents are gentle and the views from the high places are inspiring.

The Bird i' th' Hand

This is a perfect example of a purpose-built hostelry constructed alongside a turnpike road. The road was built in 1825 and linked Todmorden with Halifax via Littleborough. The pub still serves travellers and the lunchtime menu is varied and mouth-watering. The evening menu is also well worth waiting for and substantial portions of locally-produced food are served. Those in search of tea, coffee, soft drinks and sandwiches will not be disappointed either. Telephone: 01706 378145.

THE WALK

From the car park lay-by near the **Bird i' th' Hand** cross the A6033 and turn right. In around 50 yards turn left along a narrow lane indicating **Warland Gate End** and the **Pennine Way**. Follow the narrow road passing attractive cottages to the left and descend towards the **Rochdale canal**.

At **Warland**, cross the canal over a swing bridge. To the left are some locks and a marker stone indicating the position of the Lancashire/Yorkshire border.

The Rochdale canal, built during the 1790s, ran for around 30 miles between Manchester and Sowerby Bridge. Because the Pennines undulate, some 92 locks had to be built.

From **Warland Bridge** turn sharp right along an obvious track. The ascent is steep in places and passes some houses and crosses two stiles. The route also passes close to a number of pretty streams.

At **Warland Reservoir**, turn left and follow the bank.

Take time, however, to explore the wildlife on and around the water. Initially the reservoir was built to provide water for the canal but, now that there is less traffic along this cut, the supply is linked to the demands of the Rochdale area.

At the northern end of the reservoir, cross a footbridge over a feeder stream. Continue towards but do not cross a second bridge. Here, turn sharp left and, in around ½ mile, **Gaddings Dam** is reached on the right. Pass the **Basin Stone** on the left.

Drive and Stroll

The Rochdale canal at Warland

This is so named because of its shape. In the 18th century the stone was a focus for gatherings of non-conformist preachers who wished to avoid the persecution of the Church of England zealots.

(5)

Turn sharp left at a junction and descend the old packhorse route of **Salter Rake**. As its name implies this was an important trade route bringing salt from the deposits in Cheshire to all points north. Lime and coal were carried in the opposite direction. Take time here to enjoy magnificent moorland views.

(6)

At **North Hollingworth Farm**, ignore the track to the right leading to

Todmorden and continue straight ahead. The obvious and wide footpath sweeps right and then left to the tiny hamlet of **Bottomley**.

(7)

At **Bottomley** bear sharp right and, in around 300 yards, reach the **Rochdale Canal**. Cross the bridge over the canal and turn left. Follow the towpath to **Warland** and then right along **Warland Gate End** to the starting point.

Away to the left is Steanor Bottom Toll House, one of the best preserved of these structures to be found in Britain. This was set at a crossroads and its shape and windows allowed the keeper to see all the traffic and open the gates to cut delays to a minimum.